Teach Me To Fly

SUZANNE GRENELL

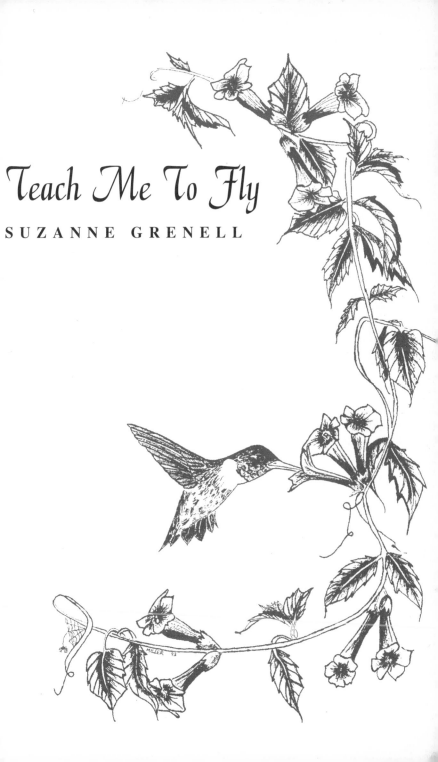

Published by: Wings As Eagles Press
            7924 East Chaparral Road
            Suite 104
            Scottsdale, Arizona 85250

Artist: Sandy Hadden Miller
Cover design and digital imaging: Gerry Dombek

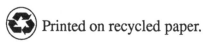 Printed on recycled paper.

ISBN 0-9637632-8-8

Teach Me To Fly

Teach me how to fly

High

So I can clearly see
The earth's beauty
And the moon's
Loyalty.

Teach me to think.

Thought

Has the universe
To play in
And freely roam in.

Teach me to learn.

New knowledge
Is discovered
When existing knowledge
Is explored.

Teach me wisdom.
So I can look at the sky
And understand
Why?

Teach me the beauty of

Stark

Stark

Simplicity.

I can feel
A single touch.

Teach me to be creative.

Write
On the paper
And paint
On the canvas
Of my mind.

Teach me to invent.

Not every color
Has been created
Or named.

Teach me to create

Images in my mind

That heal

Instead of hurt.

Teach me compassion.

If I touch someone weaker
Someone stronger
Will touch me.

Teach me to look up
At the infinite
Limitless
Countless
Endless
Boundless
Numberless
Number of stars

To understand what I can be.

If there's room to move and grow
In the universe
Then there's also room
On earth.

Teach me to seek new challenges
And never
Never.
Turn away...
Even if the space walk
Looks hard.

If I can see the star
I can get there.

Teach me to be confident.

Confidence
Breeds
Confidence.

Teach me to walk into the

Unknown.

Each step I take
Creates light.

Teach me to take risks.

If I fly
Without a parachute

Maybe I'll discover
What angels
Have known all along.

Teach me to be dangerous.
Dangerously exciting.

Because...
Boring is just so
Boring.
Predictable is just so
Predictable.
Routine is just so
Routine.
Repetition is just so
Repetitive.

Life is riskier than this.
Or it should be.

Teach me to float
In the clouds
When I need to get away
From the pressure
Of crowds...

So I can lift myself
Up
When I feel like
A limp blade of grass
Trying to stand
Under a sea of feet.

Teach me to be independent.

Like the planets
We travel with each other
As we move together
Through time
And the universe.

But also like the planets
We journey along our own paths
Created
By design
Just for us.

Teach me to transcend time...
To live two hundred years
On a page in a book
Or with letters in a manuscript
Or walk into a painting
And stay there forever
With the colors
The people
The moments
The scenes
Which are gone
But still timelessly alive
Living
Today
On the face of the canvas.

Teach me to understand
Death
Only means we've walked into
A different room.

And we will see each other again.
Somewhere
Sometime
In some other place.

And that room you walked into...
I hope it's in a mansion.

So there's room for me, too
When I reunite with you.

Teach me to forgive.

Maybe
You didn't mean to
Hurt me.

Or even if you did
Maybe
The wind will blow on
And heal
My wounds.

Teach me to bounce back

Quickly

When my life is like a ball

Flying high

Then low

On a tennis court...

Carrying my emotions

With it in the air.

Victory

Is just one more swing

Or bounce

Away.

Teach me your purpose
In allowing this to happen.

Show me
This anguishing experience
As you see it.
Let me see with your eyes
All of the good
Already born because of it

Which even now
During this fraction of a second
Is bursting into life...
Like new leaves on a tree
Planted by rivers of water.

Teach me the power
Of your healing touch.

When I am sick
You stand beside me
Guarding me
And protecting me
Like an army
Of ten thousand...

And no harm
Or evil
Can break through
The wall and the strength
Of your love.

Teach me to rise
And confidently
Walk forward again
After I take a hard fall
In sadness and in pain.
Show me the light
At midnight
And remind me
That dawn
Is always faithful.

Teach me to cry.
To feel
Deeply
Means I'm alive.

And someday...
I will walk on the water
Of my tears.

Teach me to heal
Quickly.

Touch me
With your compassion.
Take each broken piece
And make me complete.

Teach me to walk on

A carpet of stars...

Because they will turn night

Into light.

Teach me

And help me to remember

That pain

Is always temporary.

Teach me that even in the midst

Of sorrow

You can still make me laugh.

Teach me to depend on you
When it's a dry, dry
Parched
Empty
Season.

When I am a desert...
You are my sea.

Teach me to ask for help

When I can't find
The last puzzle piece.

Teach me how to calm the storms
When angry, wild waves are
Relentlessly
Restlessly
Carelessly
Ceaselessly
Churning, smashing, smashing
Churning, churning, smashing
Over and over and over again
Against my heart and head.
Right behind the rampant rage
God is blowing
Today's tempest away
And tomorrow...
It will fade into yesterday.

Teach me that this, too, will pass.

Like a shadow slowly disappearing
As the sun catches and touches it.

Like an early morning dew draping
Itself over soft flower petals.

Like a breeze gently flying
Through the air with the birds.

Like a breath of air
In the lifetime of eternity.

This, too, will pass.

Teach me to look at a rainbow
And realize that I, too,
Can stand up
And reach up
After a storm
With greater heights of energy
And brilliant bursts of intensity.

Because my heart
Is still alive.
It survived
The sultry, swirling storm...
And so did I.

Teach me to be
As strong as a flower
Growing effortlessly
Under windy
Or still
Skies

Blowing out of the earth
Like a whale
Blowing on the sea's surface

So it can give
To each day.

Teach me to have fun.

Laughter

Heals.

Teach me to find joy
In sight and sound
So whatever the circumstance...
I can see and hear
Angels playing harps.

Teach me to not look
Behind me.
Because yesterday
Is over
And walking backwards
Is slow
And thinking in the past
Prevents the future
From unfolding.

Teach me to not worry

About yesterdays

Already permanently gone.

Tomorrow's canvas is new

And different

Even more beautiful

Colors

Can be chosen.

Teach me to wait
When I have to.

It might take time
To perfect
But so does any
Great work of art.

Teach me to have patience.

Spring always follows
Winter.

Someday...
I will find a flower
Where once there was only snow.

Teach me faith.

Logic

Is too logical

For the force

Of a miracle

Moving faster

Than the fastest

Thought.

Teach me to hope

So I can expect

Something much greater

Than capability

Or circumstance.

Teach me how to pray
And to remember
It's not at all difficult.

Even now
You can clearly hear
My every thought.

You understand my words
Before I even think them.

Teach me to run
With your wind
On my back...
And in my spirit.

So each breath I take
And each step I take
Is stronger.

Teach me to be quiet
In the motionless stillness
Of the night
So I can hear
My thoughts...
And yours.

Teach me to listen.

Even silence

Speaks.

Teach me to look for you
And find comfort
When I'm feeling
Comfortless.

Lift me up
And hold me high and close
When I step on a thorn
Or dash my naked foot
Or soul against a stone.

Let me feel
Let me know
The strong and soothing power
Of your presence.

Teach me to not be afraid
Of veiled demons in the dark
Who sometimes surround me
With their heavy
Pressing presence.

I know I am strong
With the strength
Of your strength.

Teach me to believe.

Life is so much more
Than what we can see.

And even if we go to the
Edge
Of the earth's horizon...
We're not going to fall off.

Teach me the power of truth.

Speak it to me

In a promise

And show me

How truth comes true.

Teach me to write
So I can describe
The mystery and majesty
Of you
Exploding into
My unbounded fascination
With you.

So bring the letters together
And let them
Press and touch and turn
Until they draw deep breaths
On their own

And call out your name.

Teach me to discover

You

So you will discover

Me.

Teach me what you know.

Your mind is more brilliant than

The most profound literature

Ever written

Since the beginning

Of the beginning

Of thought

And more exciting

Than leaping between two stars

In one jump

Higher than the height of heaven.

Teach me to reveal to you
Just how much
I am thinking about you.
Let me silently
Touch your spirit.

I prayed for you today.
Could you tell?
You must have known.

For God wouldn't have laid you
On my heart
If he didn't want to touch you
With his.

Teach me the force
Of your love.

Your energy
And intensity
Are drawing me into
Your magnetic field...

A spinning, spiral galaxy
Of deep
Electrifying
Exciting
Excitement.

Teach us to love each other.

Together.

One complete love.

Because half a love

Is empty and hollow.

Incomplete.

Like wind without air.

So blow your love on both of us

In the same breath

And create in us a concert

Of rhythms running together

And rhymes that never part.

Teach me to express to you the
Feelings my heart feels for you.

More than the 5.88 trillion miles
That light travels in one year
As it skips through the universe...
And more than all of the galaxies
With their billions and billions
Of stars
That decorate and illuminate
The night skies
Like a chandelier...

That's how much I love you
And need you.

Teach me to love
Passionately
But with wisdom.

Teach me to sleep

Deep

So I can close my eyes

And dream a dream for you.

Visit me in my mind

Play a part in the night play

I promise you an audience

I'll watch you on the stage.

And even in the morning light

With the blast of a new day

I promise you, my star and love

You'll never fade away.

Teach me to be close to you

Even when we are apart.

I miss you today.

I hope you miss me, too...

So you can hold me

In your mind

And whisper to me

In thought.

Teach me to not feel lonely.
I looked for you today
But I did not find you.
I called out your name
But you did not answer.
I reached out for you
But I could not feel your touch.

Even so
A thousand angels heard me
And with a thousand voices
Surrounded me
And sang
Just to me
A song.

Teach me to look at the moon
And feel close to you.

Because I know
That wherever you are
You can see it, too...

Teach me all that can happen

In one

Just one

Brief but brilliant blink

In eternity.

Teach me to communicate to you

The treasure I have found in you.

For from the moment we met

You have given me

More excitement than life's

Greatest mystery

And my friendship with you

Will be recorded eternally

On the golden pages

Of earth's and heaven's history

To live forever timelessly

In the new world you created

For me...

Full of everlasting majesty.

Teach me to ask you
To come with me
To jump
High
And then jump again
Even higher
On the earth's
Giant trampoline.

Together
We can forget every care
And use our momentum
To keep us in the air.

Teach me how to make

Each minute we share

Greater

Than the minute before

And so much less

Than the minute to come.

Teach me to move
With the movement
Of two clouds
Dancing across open skies

And never let anything
Trap
My freedom to be free.

Boundaries and fences
Only exist
If I allow them
To be built.

Teach me to soar

Across clear, quiet, open skies

That reach without effort

Into

Vast

Unexplored

Light-years............................

So I can discover

Something new

In tomorrow.

Teach me to expect
Surprises.
And even then...

Surprise me.

Teach me to live each day
Like it's one day longer
Than I expected to have...

And to live
In this moment
Because this moment
Is living
In me.

Teach me to slow down
Once in awhile
And escape from
Time
Clocks
Schedules
Watches.

Today
I just feel like
Watching the birds

And for awhile
Becoming one of them.